A BOUNTY OF
PASSING MOMENTS

A Bounty of Passing Moments

REFLECTIONS ON DANCE AND WORSHIP

❖❖❖❖❖❖❖❖❖❖❖❖❖❖❖❖❖❖❖❖❖❖❖❖❖❖❖❖❖

MARGARET STEVENS

Signed for Audrey with best wishes

Margaret

SHEFFIELD
CAIRNS PUBLICATIONS
1994

ISBN 1 870652 20 7

First published 1994

Further copies of this book are obtainable from
Cairns Publications
47 Firth Park Avenue, Sheffield S5 6HF

*Printed by J.W. Northend Ltd
Clyde Road, Sheffield S8 0TZ*

Contents

v

Preface

If it had not been for my friend Nadia Kevan, this book would never have appeared. In 1989 she persuaded me that some account of my experience in dance and worship would be of interest to a number of people. She interviewed me with a tape recorder running and then transcribed our conversation. The result has needed considerable editing, and what you have in front of you is a selection derived from that transcript.

Then Jim Cotter suggested I should interweave my reflections with quotations that have inspired me. I hope you will find they illuminate as well as echo the themes that matter to me so passionately.

I have not told a story that is continuous over the past thirty years, but felt it best to share some of the insights I have gained from that experience. But they come much more from everything I have been given by those who have worked with me.

I wish I could name them all, but I must mention John Brassington by name as well as Nadia. In a way he provides the story line by telling of The St Michael's Dancers at Coventry Cathedral. I am grateful to him, as I am also to Laurence Reading, who has contributed a generous Foreword. Sister Theresa Margaret OHN has helped the book to dance by her drawings. My appreciation and thanks to her.

So many people have opened doors for me, loved and

supported me, and put up with me. What can I say that would be enough? I have such a deep sense of gratitude to all those who have made my dreams of sacred dance come true. Without their dedication this small book would never have been offered.

MARGARET STEVENS
Holt, Norfolk, February 1994

Foreword

Would you mind if we opened a window? It will, of course, let in the air, and probably the light, and will bring movement and change the feel of things.

Margaret Stevens, in her pioneering work with dance in worship has done something very like this. Her reflections and meditations on her experiences form a fascinating and revealing account of the ways in which this opening up has influenced their understanding of worship for many people.

That so much has been achieved, gently and without publicity, is evidence of her combination of skill and charm, backed by a quiet determination. The discipline which is the essential mark of a dancer has provided the underlying strength which has often surprised those who were unaware of the depth of commitment and knowledge which the work involved. Theological and scriptural understanding are not usually thought to be connected with an imaginative use of movement and colour, and the rightful part the body plays in worship. To have brought them together with music and poetry has given worship a new vision and depth.

Margaret Stevens' courage and ability in opening up the possibilities of a creative use of dance in worship have been highly valued by those who have worked with her or who have entered more deeply into prayer because of the dances they have seen. This small volume, which I know she wants to point to the Dance rather than to her, will encourage others to follow in her steps.

Laurence Reading
Witham, Essex, February 1994

*Reflections on
Dance and Worship*

Reflections on Dance and Worship

One interesting thing about the dancers was that they belonged to different churches or to none. It was of no concern to me what their allegiance was. Indeed I didn't find out for some time that the group consisted of Roman Catholics, Baptists, Quakers, Anglicans, Methodists – and one Buddhist. Perhaps the very fact that they were dancing showed that they were still on a journey to where they truly belonged. Why, in any case, should we need to have a label to say how special we are? When I lived in an ecumenical community, visitors always asked us which church we belonged to, as though we ought to be wearing T-shirts with a label across the front. What mattered was that we were human beings – Christian, agnostic, frail, saintly, ordinary, working and living together with the same vision and ideals.

MARGARET STEVENS

I remember some years ago watching a wren sing in the garden. It was perched on the clothes line, and as it sang its whole body wobbled with the intensity of its song. It was so small compared with the volume of sound it poured out for all to hear.

This is my model for theology. The first noticeable

thing about it is how the wren sang. Every part of itself was used. None of it was uninvolved in its song. It did not use just its throat and beak, or its head. Every feather was aquiver; every blood vessel throbbed; every muscle was stretched.

The same is true of theology. Of speaking about God. All of us who do this speak with the whole of what we are: our bodies, our blood, our emotions, our nerves. Every glance, every intake of breath, and every joke we share is part of what we say. Theology is not a disembodied exercise for spiritual fitness freaks; neither is it an activity for headless wonders. It is an expression of our total engagement, body, mind, and spirit, in what it means to be alive and human, just as the wren is totally engaged in its singing.

We are also too small for what we sing, not only because we always mean more than we can say, but because God, the subject of our song, cannot be contained within the measure of our voice. Therefore it is important, if our theology is to emanate from the spirit of truth, that we are prepared to listen to different songs.

Anna Primavesi

A song in the rain.
   As if the sound were washing
      all with its music

clean, and praise the Lord!
   In a chatter of raindrops
      one singer exults –

a Song-Thrush, feathers
　　fluffed to let it feel the rain,
　　　coming as near bare

as a fledged bird can.
　　Blossom bounces on the trees
　　　at the drumming rain,

all – it seems to me –
　　shaking with soundless laughter.
　　　Daybreaking delight.

A lad in the rain
　　laughing. Old Mother Matson
　　　beyond the window,

angry. I want more.
　　Not enough to feel big drops
　　　bouncing on my cheeks;

I want the rain
　　to tickle me to laughing
　　　aloud with my joy,

to be drenched with it,
　　my feet in loud splashing sprays
　　　as I dance in it.

If only I dare.
　　"Tha'rt dancin' i't'Devil's game.
　　　God weren'd forgive the'!"

…to be naked…Ah!
　　And dancing. To make God laugh.
　　　If only I'd dared.

HAROLD MORLAND

A rather grand luncheon club invited me to speak to them about my work as a magistrate. But I was much more excited by a new venture with a small dance group, and I replied that I would talk about dance or not come at all. The offer was accepted, and, greatly daring, I took my dancers with me.

I gave a talk on dance being a different response to life, to nature, and to music – and to one another and to God. The last dance we did was to music from Handel's *Messiah*. I can't think how I had the nerve to do it. But the dance was met, not with clapping, but with a beautiful dense silence.

Afterwards somebody commented to me, "You should do that in church." Now this was over thirty years ago when such a thing was unheard of – even if dance flourished as part of worship in the Middle Ages and even later. I replied that that was indeed how I saw it: when I'd heard music in church I'd danced in my head many times. But I couldn't imagine anyone allowing it. "Well," she said, "leave it to me – you never know."

Before long an invitation came. Tentatively, the vicar of a church said he would try it – but he wouldn't advertise it and he wouldn't make it part of the usual service. So we had to wait until after Evensong (which was very dull!). Anyway, we danced. We wore clothes with little tops we had made for ourselves. It all looked pleasant enough, but there was nothing spectacular. At the end of the dance we gave each person in the congregation a flower.

One person who was there happened to be involved with Southwark Cathedral. And the next invitation came from there. In almost seventeen years we never had to ask to go anywhere. There was always somebody at one place who asked us to the next.

MARGARET STEVENS

What kind of place lends itself to the dancing of the Magnificat or the Mass? I believe with the Quakers and many others that anywhere can be a sacred place and any meal a sacrament. But a visual art like dance is helped by different architectural shapes and textures, and by the colour and atmosphere of the building. And there is atmosphere in places where people have prayed much.

So I have always walked round a church, looking at it and sensing its 'quality' before accepting an invitation to dance there. I wanted to feel it and make friends with it, so that the dance could reflect the building and the building reflect the dance.

Not that I haven't danced elsewhere. I remember one occasion with the Sufis, for example, in Caxton Hall. But I never felt quite the same about it. I think this is because halls are places for performances rather than for acts of worship. If you are dancing part of the service, the dance flows out of what has gone before it and into what comes after it. If you have been dancing Jacob's dream, and it ends on the words, "Surely the Lord is in this place," the energy of the dance can be caught up in the celebrant declaring, "The Lord is here."

MARGARET STEVENS

If we are truly to regenerate our idea of sacred space then we need to recognize, with Peter Brook, that what we are looking for is 'empty space', the space where re-creative divine love can, but will not necessarily, manifest itself in judgment and mercy. How? If we take up Brook's criticism of Coventry Cathedral (that "ceremony in all its meanings…should have dictated the shape of the place…the outer form can only take on real authority if the ceremony has equal authority") I think we could make a start by…making a space for sacred dance. We cannot any longer think about sacred space within a church context without giving space for the circle dance, and indeed all other forms of dance. Dance is holy, as the feminist movement has rediscovered, because the body is holy, and it celebrates the body. A theology of creation cannot do without it.

TIM GORRINGE

We rarely moved any of the furnishings in churches where we danced. I wanted the congregation to feel that they were actually with us and weren't sitting back thinking it was all lovely, just like the ballet on television. I wanted them to recognize themselves and to think, "I could do that!" So anything theatrical wasn't right for us. We used almost no make-up, no jewelry, no fancy dresses or hair styles. About the only unusual part of our appearance was our bare feet!

   Once in a while we needed some kind of platform at the chancel step simply so that people could see. But we preferred to make a lot of use of the aisles so that people could sense we belonged to them and that we weren't doing anything stagey.

MARGARET STEVENS

For the last few months I have stood by this miracle of perfection (the Parthenon) wrought by human hands. I did not dare move, for I realized that of all the movements my body had made, none was worthy to be made before a Doric Temple. And as I stood, this I realized, that I must find a dance whose effect was worthy of this temple, or never dance again. For many days no movement came to me, and then one day came the thought, These columns which seem so straight are not really straight. Each one is curving gently from the base to the height, each one is in flowing movement, never resting, and the movement of each is in harmony with the others. As I thought this my arms rose slowly towards the temple and I leaned forward. I had found my dance; it was a prayer.

ISADORA DUNCAN

No trace of a master plan has ever been found. If you look around, you can see where the builders have improvised. In the South Transept, they never brought their arches straight down on the capitals, they are always a bit out. It gives a sense of life and movement you don't find in a church where every stone was laid with mathematical precision.

LIBRARIAN of Westminster Abbey

One particular vicar didn't want the group to dance; he wanted me to teach the people of the parish to dance. It was a parish on a huge housing estate, with the biggest bingo hall in England. The church too was large, built of red brick in the thirties. And the first people I met didn't exactly look as if they wanted to dance in church! But I accepted the invitation and I went there every week for a long time.

They were certainly enthusiastic. And I wasn't the only 'teacher' recruited by the vicar. He had decided that his people could do anything that anybody else could do. He got Constance Spry to teach them how to arrange flowers, musicians to teach them about music, artists to teach them about the visual arts. When I told one of my sons about this particular church, I said, "They are such ordinary people." He replied, "And what are *you*?"

MARGARET STEVENS

It is so difficult to communicate the magic moments. I would be demonstrating a movement, and then I would turn round. And 'it' had happened. People were dancing. They had been liberated. Such moments cannot be shared afterwards: they are precious but they cannot last. They are moments of rapture. You can't expect them, you can't make them happen, but once in a while they do.

MARGARET STEVENS

Warm, outflowing joy, unmarred by turbulence
Of agitated disbelief:
Freedom to smile, and breathe
The glory of sheer being, all the dance
Of nature's easy rhythm in my blood.
O gentle life in which I freely move,
No longer watching with a blank regard
My shadow move ineptly through the maze,
Stumbling and shuddering at every touch.
O ardent air, O limpid tender seas
That bathe and heal with all the power of love.
How should I answer this, God's matchless gift,
But with the exultation of my heart?

SR BENEDICTA, SSC

I can't understand how it is that dance touches people's hearts so. And in a way I don't want to understand it because I believe there should always be some mystery. And people cry when they are touched by it. They are so involved. Let it remain a mystery.

MARGARET STEVENS

The world breaks everyone and afterwards many are strong in the broken places.

ERNEST HEMINGWAY

For God hath made you able to create worlds in your own mind, which are more precious to Him than those which He created.

THOMAS TRAHERNE

Since I have been dancing I have felt my heart slowly melting away some of the ice, and love and joy growing. It has also spilled over into my work and home. Some of the 'magic' will linger for a long time.

CHERYL COOKE

❖

One criticism has come to me from those involved in the charismatic movement. They do not think I allow the Holy Spirit to take over the body and move it. But what concerns me about their services is that their movements are repetitive and limited in their range, mostly with the arms. Now if you have been liberated by a particular experience of release in a charismatic group, I suppose it is difficult to believe that the Holy Spirit can work through choreography.

At one workshop we had a couple of charismatic

people who were arguing in this way. Some of the others in the group responded that they hadn't been released until they had known what they were doing. They needed safety and clear shapes and boundaries before they were able to trust the Spirit. They needed to know the vocabulary of dance before they could be free in the use of its language.

In the middle of the discussion one woman, sitting on a garden bench, said, "I don't know why you are all talking like this. Quite simply, dancing in church has changed my life."

MARGARET STEVENS

You spoke about daring, but I do not think you should be afraid to be more daring if you wish, when the place and occasion seem right. Out of season it might retard timid people's openness to the art of dance at the altar. The cardinal question is, I think, whether the daring theological thought needs to be put over, and if so, what is the best artistic idiom for it. Or perhaps whether some accepted idea has become stale and needs a daring idiom to bring it back to life. For one can be daring in content or in idiom or in both. I believe a congregation deep down will accept what is daring to them if they feel sure you are sincere. They may not like it, but they will think about it. Sometimes of course, in drama, an audience denounces what it does not wish to accept, in defensive anger. We all agree that we must not gloat then, but we need not be ashamed if we think this is the reason for the hostility. Our Lord seems to have given some offence; we cannot claim his assurance of right-eousness, but we can surely be forgiven for sometimes not foreseeing all the reactions.

GRAHAM SUTER

The mind of a philosopher should aim to be like a good dancer. The chief character of good dancing is the union of the maximum of energetic movement with the maximum of well-balanced grace. The whole muscular system is alive to restrain any excess, so that however wild and free the movement may seem, it is always measured. Excess would mean ignominious collapse.

HAVELOCK ELLIS

It is costly to dance in church – or anywhere else for that matter. You are vulnerable because in your move-ments you are revealing yourself in a way that you can hide in speech, writing, painting, music. I think it is this vulnerability which touches people quite deeply, both those who see the dance and those who take part in it. And this willingness to be vulnerable is what begins to change you.

Most of those who have danced with me acknowledge that the life of the spirit – however you might describe it – is important to them. Otherwise I don't think they would become involved. They aren't exactly pursuing their careers, and they soon learn that dancing truthfully is the opposite of showing off. And the 'Spirit' does change people through the dance.

I don't know whether the dance makes a great difference to the details of people's daily lives, but I do think it makes a difference to their relationships with one another and with God – and very often with music and with nature.

MARGARET STEVENS

My passing from this world will leave no mark. Those who loved me may grieve but I hope not for long. I will leave nothing remarkable for this world to wonder at, but the world has given me its riches. My eyes have feasted on great beauty, my ears have heard beautiful sounds. I have smelt the delights of many places, tasted several delicacies. I have touched others and they have touched me, and my body has strolled, leapt, blundered, rushed, wandered, and marched on through this life. I have danced.

WENDY BUNN

As people begin to change, they start feeling all kinds of emotions, not least the sorrows of life. And I think people should be free to cry when they need to. It is important in rehearsal that the group should stop dancing when someone's tears are released. We don't crowd a person, but we do gather round. And of course dancers touch. It comes very easily to us. And people who have never experienced touch, except perhaps sexually, now experience tenderness. So we let one another cry; sometimes even cry with them. We never say, "Don't cry." I remember one occasion when one member of the group told us she had faced a cot death. We cried, and we danced about death.

MARGARET STEVENS

Your dancers were moving (in both senses) although some moved more easily than others. There were three dancers whom I found especially beautiful: the tall woman with short dark hair I felt was totally immersed in her dance and 'in touch' with the others. The two young women with long hair also caught my eye. I could see, on the other hand, one or two who were 'going through the motions' but were afraid of their bodies and didn't dare touch their fellow dancers.

Touch is so very important. It gives us warmth and shelter, and, I believe, allows us to share our energy and love with one another. But it does take time before we can let go and allow another person to come in.

GRAHAM HILL

We never finished either a rehearsal or a dance in a service on a tense note. We would end cheerfully or peacefully. Now there is a danger in this because everyone goes away feeling marvellous. So I remind people that they are going to feel awful the next day unless they get down to making a cake or doing something else ordinary and practical.

Margaret Stevens

Beauty is not the starting point but the point of arrival. A thing can be beautiful if it is true. Truth itself is only a complete harmony, and harmony is finally only a bundle of utilities. The miracle of life could not be perpetuated but for the constant renewal of universal balance.

Auguste Rodin

I became involved with in-service training for clergy of the Church of England. On one occasion I was faced with a group of sixteen men from inner-city parishes, none of whom had any experience of dance. I remember one of them saying, "If you ask me to do press-ups I will." He looked like a Welsh rugby forward! They were all diffident – probably the shyest group I ever had. But because I came to dance when I was fifty or so and felt that for the first time my life I was sounding the right note, and because I was an older person anyway, I didn't threaten them. I was even able to have a laugh with the rugby forward because I have great big rugby-playing sons. But it helped to call what we did movement rather than dance – it seemed less frightening! Since they knew the Bible, it was then but a small step to translate into movement words like, "Then shall the eyes of the blind be opened, and the ears of the deaf unstopped."

MARGARET STEVENS

The human body, in its occupation of space, communicates much without words. The physical deportment of liturgical ministers is therefore of great importance: it should be relaxed and natural without suggesting informality, gracefully formal without being stiff or rigid. The problem with many liturgical ministers is not that their bodies say too little but that they say too much and say it badly. In processions ministers 'march' in clots as though clinging to each other for comfort or support rather than spacing themselves well so that their movement takes on a modest significance. A procession is a parade, not a bus queue. Liturgical body language is an art of great understatement, and as such requires physical discipline. The marks of the chisel should never show.

AIDAN KAVANAGH

We seem to have forgotten that we share with the rest of the human race that the first movement of dance – from crawling on all fours to standing on two feet – such a movement reflects beautifully the belief that we are all created to reflect the divine image.

DONALD REEVES

A lot of people use their bodies simply to carry their heads around. They don't even use their bodies – they use a car! But just to lift one's hands in prayer is to start to be a praying body. A lot of prayer and worship could develop from that and become more dance-like. Have a look at the way in which celebrants of Holy Communion use their hands. Their gestures can look meaningless. The words, "Lift up your hearts," are often accompanied by two hands held stiffly like sticks going up in the air. "Peace be with you" is a bidding which needs a gesture of arms opening from the very centre of the person's being.

People may need to be taught this – except that we know it already but need to be reminded of it. If you are going to meet your child from school you don't look up in a book of words how to do it. You bend down and open your arms and the child runs into them. So we are talking about something that is perfectly natural. It is such a pity that we have lost that sense of gesture and movement in worship. What usually happens is that people stand up and sit down and kneel (or crouch) without any awareness of how these movements can themselves be part of prayer. If you kneel down in a pew you can see only heads – and children disappear altogether.

Of course you have to be careful in introducing movement to a congregation. You have to make sure that nobody feels second class because they don't or can't join in. At first you need to be simple and straightforward, avoiding any suggestions that might cause embarrassment. "How are you sitting? Are you conscious that both your feet are on the ground? Is your head being held properly on your spine? Are your hands resting gently on your lap? Shall we do that together?" You need do no more than that to sense your body as centred and stable, head and trunk all of a piece. Then you can say, "Look at your hands. What have they done today? They are given to you by God. They can express greed – clench them – or they can express generosity – open them." Anybody can do that – and it is the beginning of dance.

MARGARET STEVENS

Dance is most natural, graceful and fitting when liturgy takes the imagination seriously. When the setting is right, when a church building looks as if a celebration is going to happen, when everything that is said, through images and stories, appeals to the imagination as well as to reason, when the church smells right – incense or other sorts of fragrance – when all these are in place, then it would be odd if there were no music, no dance.

And by imagination I mean that faculty in all human beings which gathers our experience in such a way as to provoke meaning and hope.

DONALD REEVES

Next to the human face, hands are perhaps the most expressive parts of the human body. Their choreography runs the gamut of all human attitudes and emotions, as one can see in iconography and in classical ballet. In the liturgy one can see hands spread for prayer, folded in devotion, gracefully extended in invitation, and tracing signs of indication and blessing.

AIDAN KAVANAGH

One of the problems about dance being used in worship is that the leader of a group has to have a special combination of talents. She has to have some theological knowledge and to have done some reading about the theme to be portrayed. She has to be able to train people and choreograph a sequence of movement. The group has to be willing to be trained enough to present a piece really well.

Because of all this preparation, it is more likely that a dance is presented at a festival than at any other time. There are plenty of opportunities for dancing for your own refreshment, but to do it on behalf of a congregation demands dedication. You have to be careful not to be like the self-conscious amateur actor who can't lose himself in the role he is playing. Otherwise those watching will be thinking of the actor as a person and not of the play. A really professional group of dancers will of course be very polished in what they present. But there is nothing wrong in the slight roughness of less skilled groups. It can even be quite touching and involve the hearts of the congregation more. What is vital is love and sincerity and care about the people who are there and the giving of one's best.

The marvellous thing is that such dance is spreading – one or two permanent groups and a number that get together for special occasions. We mustn't let 'experts' take over everything in our lives. And our desire and ability to dance is so fundamental to the living through of our sorrows and joys.

MARGARET STEVENS

To take pleasure in God's creation means to express delight in the sensual and the erotic. Eroticism usually means sexual sensation and gratification. It is thus cut off from the intensity of feelings which in loving relationships (well beyond sexual ones) becomes its true meaning. This is the intensity of feelings of self-worth, and of being valued, of our interdependence, of nothingness and pain, of tenderness and of anger, of our amazing capacity to create change, and of the possibilities of intimacy.

And Dance is a natural vehicle for this pleasure to be expressed.

DONALD REEVES

There is no real split between living and dancing. To become aware of dance is to learn how to move and live well. There is a close connection between what is natural and correct for the body and the ability to use it as an instrument of expression. If your body is right and your spirit is right you are walking on air. You aren't making any footprints in the sand. Everything seems to be right. It isn't God's will that we be hunched up and tense. We need to use only that part of the body that is expressing what we want to say: the rest should be free of tension.

MARGARET STEVENS

Form is necessary to matter, to shape and give security to the soul, which is fearful of too much reality. But the soul may be stunted if it lives only a narrow and enclosed life, never realizing that there is something larger into which it could be released. The 'led life' in houses, the habitual patterns of family and social behaviour, and the structuring of identity around the ego give form and security at the expense of illumination.

On the other hand, a life which is rooted, which has an organic form, derived from growing in one spot, does possess a spiritual value, which those who have given themselves over to the quest for 'freedom' lose.

Although the cell of the body and of the led life must be transcended, it is not necessary, or even desirable, to uproot oneself completely. Flux, expressed in images of water, fire, and wind, is all around and exists also in the soul. One only has to open one's eyes.

PATRICK WHITE

If you dance the theme of peace without dancing chaos first, you don't get interesting choreography. Subjects like darkness and light, or the binding of imprisonment and the freedom of release, give a lot of colour to what you are doing as well as relating to an experience that other people can understand.

We danced for Amnesty International in Westminster Abbey. We had an Amnesty candle unlit and surrounded with barbed wire, and we placed it in the middle of the chancel steps. The prisoners came in accompanied by their captors – who never looked at them. (Is it true that if you steadily look a person in the eyes, compassion is stirred within you?) To dance despair – and to watch people dancing despair – is to know what it is like much more than if you simply read about despair.

The climax of the dance was the prisoners' forgiveness of their persecutors and the lighting of the candle. The prisoners weren't set free, yet the Spirit of freedom was clearly at work. If you love God and are killed, that is a tragedy. But it is a far greater tragedy if you kill somebody in anger and either you are not forgiven or you aren't able to receive forgiveness.

MARGARET STEVENS

They shall all come, and you too shall come,
My people shall come, and hell shall be harrowed.
I touch you, I touch you, the Spirit is running
To you, and through you, the tongues are descending.
You cannot escape them and No shall be Yes and
Yes shall be No, and hell shall be harrowed.
And hell shall be harrowed. I touch you, I touch you

And through you, and to you, I weave in between you.
The blind are seeing, the lame are dancing,
And light is ascending,
The Spirit is running, the darkness is ending.

THOMAS BLACKBURN

As far as I can remember, we have never danced anything just because it looked 'nice'. Every movement had a meaning so that the dancers' hearts – indeed their whole being – could be in everything they did.

In a dance like one expressing the Magnificat, the outward movement is towards God, but there is a hidden inner movement as well. There needs to be if the whole is to have meaning. And if you think about it all movement starts with stillness and finishes with stillness. The trouble is that we are so uncomfortable with stillness. We are restless people. Anxious movement is full of tension and without meaning. In most forms of worship we are never still for long – neither do we move with grace and meaning.

We move without true awareness. Look at people as they approach an altar to receive communion. They shuffle along as if they were in a queue to buy a railway ticket. Think of how this could be transformed into a beautiful slow walk, thoughtfully and wonderingly approaching the One you love most! To do that well you have to know what stillness is, and to start there.

In a dance with the *Washing of the Disciples' Feet* on Maundy Thursday there was a special use of stillness –

touching and holding and staying still. That kind of contact can be mutually healing. The touch doesn't impose itself and the person touched is freed to receive it as a gift.

MARGARET STEVENS

The liturgy itself is a complex and solemn form of communal dance, of formal motion the choreography of which is its ceremony. If one wishes to enhance the assembly's appreciation of bodily motion as a means of expressing and communicating sacred values, one might give attention to the liturgy's ceremonial choreography and to freeing the assembly from the physical restraints pews force upon it.

AIDAN KAVANAGH

See how they move with strange smooth faces now.
Their feet find sympathy they never found
In words, their joy is bouncing on the ground.
The faster that they move the more they show
Soft and impressive features. It's as though
Thought were abandoned and the mind grown small,
And we sense peace however fast they move,
Some centre they have found, silent and still,
Round which they dance. It looks like love until
The music stops, they separate and send
Shudders of betrayal through us all.

ELIZABETH JENNINGS

It is difficult to start and finish a dance in church. There is nothing at all to help you. You have to get on and you have to get off. That causes a problem, especially if you are going off and soon have to do another dance – and one of the dancers disappears into the vestry instead of the Lady Chapel. Or the next dance is in couples and you are one short – and on top of that you are supposed to put a skirt on in the chapel. Another hazard is dancing up a stone aisle and being unaware of six feet of black marble in the middle, and you skid on it. There is the hazard of gratings where you can get your big toe stuck – or someone's button falls off their fly and goes down the grating. (Yes, that actually happened.) And you have to be professional about it even if you are an amateur. It mustn't matter.

MARGARET STEVENS

At a Harvest Festival we finished with a dance at the Offertory at the Holy Communion. We carried a beautiful basket of black grapes and a sheaf of wheat. Others brought things that were a blessing to them – dressmaking equipment, bricks, flowers, tools.

On another occasion one woman said she was going to bring her handicapped son. Somehow I had lost all sense of what the dance was about and I thought it would be wrecked. It was a terrible thing for me to think. Mercifully I didn't say anything and afterwards I asked a nun in the group what she thought. She replied, "It may be a discord, but there is always discord before the final cadence." I was stunned with remorse. And when the boy did reach the altar during the dance, he lifted his arms to the vicar. Marvellous!

MARGARET STEVENS

In my dances I try and use all the senses as much as I can to communicate: through the warmth of a candle, through seeing its light, through colours, through the touch of silk. There is a simple candle dance that anybody can learn, with each person lighting a candle from the first one that is lit. What a wonderful way to celebrate Easter in the darkness before dawn after the proclamation of the Light of Christ from the newly lit Candle of the Resurrection! You can let people move as they wish during a period of improvisation, and you will find that some will keep remarkably still, often just kneeling. A variant is a dance in which you light a candle from the central one and place it in a bowl of sand, and as you do so naming somebody you want to pray for.

There are so many things you can do – wearing coloured silks round your waists and taking them off and waving them about as a way of dancing the Gloria, or using them to proclaim the Rainbow of Promise.

MARGARET STEVENS

I have always believed dance to be an art form, a means of communication, and for this you need to be able to make gestures with your body that others are able to interpret. The joy of movement comes from within, a fact I readily acknowledge. But I do not feel that a service should have an 'interlude', with the majority of those present merely onlookers while a small group praise God in their own way. If we cannot speak to and for others through our movement, then we should confine our contribution to the privacy of our weekly meetings. Perhaps it is a fault of our society that we have become observers. The media enable us to appreciate a wide range of customs and cultures and we are able to see 'the best' that art can offer. So our movement has to be pleasing to the eye if the congregation are to be drawn into sharing our joy. If it isn't pleasing, people will withdraw through embarrassment. They may admire our courage, but they won't have been led into deeper worship through our dance.

WENDY BUNN

The body has wisdom to teach that the mind knows not of. It understands much of rhythm and timing which is easily forgotten when life is ruled exclusively by ideas. Such fundamental themes as the relation between activity and passivity, strength and weakness, tension and relaxation, disease and grace, are more easily learned from bodily movement than from conceptual analysis. As Zorba knew, there are times when only dance can say what must be said. There are certain emotions which are difficult to entertain without motion. We are moved by joy and shaken by grief. It may be that the sparsity of joy in contemporary life is closely related to the loss of dance as a central vehicle for the education and articulation of values and beliefs. We do not share the same dances. Perhaps corporate bonds are forged only when bodies join together in celebration. If so, re-education of the body is essential for creating a community. Is it really possible to be in touch without touching, to be moved without moving?

SAM KEEN

I have been leading a movement class in the small town where I now live. One day I introduced a Peace Dance at the end, and it included a bit of touch. People were surprised but pleased. Of course you have to be sensitive about this, but they found they had come to the group to get thin and had gone away changed in spirit.

MARGARET STEVENS

For our life
    is but a song,

And the reason
    for our singing

Is to praise you
    for the music;

Join the dance of
    your creation.

From *Laudato Si, O mi Signore*

O God of Dance
in whom we live and move and have our being,
so direct our strength
and inspire our weakness
that we may enter with power
into the movement of your whole creation
through our partner Jesus Christ.

JANET MORLEY

Outrageous! Shouldn't be allowed! These are typical reactions to the idea of dance in worship. Yet we are not shocked by flower arrangements, singing, music, architecture, painting, stained glass, and other forms of art. The association of dance with pleasure, self-gratification, flaunting the body, eroticism, and touch results in this reaction of horror to the thought that it should be used to glorify God. We are still uneasy with any kind of touch and can be embarrassed by the Peace at the Holy Communion. Dance is for Saturday night, worship for Sunday morning. The split in Western Christianity between flesh and spirit is here in ample evidence.

Rational debate will not persuade people where emotions run high. And religious dance is an emotive issue. All we can do is invite people to experience it, to use the body more fully in worship, to let go and see whether it means something to us. We don't even have to explain that something. A famous ballerina said that if she could express what she had to say in words she wouldn't need to dance it.

KEITH PLAISTER

I want to express – Beauty – Purity – Love – above all
love in its divine sense. Art, Love, Nature are only an
infinitesimal part of God's Spirit. I want to recapture it
and give it to others so that they may know that He is
omnipresent. If they feel it then I am reflecting Him.

VASLAV NIJINSKY

Silence; equipoise; stone;
Images of age ungrown,
Slow growing of bone
In the bell-clear silence drowning noise,
Your mood, heart, body, equipoise.

Objects are, stillness breathes,
Dancers held are crisp leaves
The dead wind bequeathes,
Objects are: Rivers dammed, hair unpinned
Hanging ready in the dead wind.

You danced, you dance. All space
Shattered like a dropped glass
When from tight embrace
Bodies folded flung, flew, swam and fell;
The dancers stepped their broken spell.

Lithe dancers span and stepped,
And the new music swept
Into old, slewed, slept.
The opening spring of energy slows
And love of hidden silence grows.

And you alone dance on,
Though silence must return
And movements that shone
Put to womb again, nothing destroys.
Your dance unends in equipoise.

ANON.

O dance Diana, dance Endymion
Till calm ancestral shadows lay their hands
Gently across mine eyes; in days long gone
Have I not danced with gods in garden lands?
I too a wild unsighted atom bourne
Deep in the heart of some heroic day
Span in dance ten thousand years ago,
And while his young eyes glittered in the morn
Something of me felt something of his joy,
And longed to rule a body, and to know.

JAMES ELROY FLECKER

Human beings have worshipped knowledge, knowledge
as identified with intellect. The erudite person, the
scholar, the philosopher, the inventor, the scientist, are
all concerned with knowledge and have created marvellous things in the world. Their knowledge is overwhelm-
ing: we marvel and accept it. So we have developed an
inordinate admiration for the intellect. This applies to
sacred books and their interpretations. In contrast to

that there is a reaction to being emotional, having feelings, to love, to have devotion, extravagance of expression. And the body is neglected. This division between body, mind and spirit is unnatural. We have to bring about a natural harmony where the intellect functions like a marvellous watch; where the emotions, affections, care, love and compassion are healthily functioning. And the body which has been so misused can come into its own.

JIDDU KRISHNAMURTI

[There were protests at a Mass with dance at the French Church off Leicester Square in London in June 1973. One protester had managed to shout, "This is a pantomime," before being escorted out.]

There was a unifying effect on the congregation who had already been invited to make simple gestures of offering at the Offertory. "Lord, let me see these hands as you see them. When I am angry – *clenched fists* – bring me peace – *hands folded together*; when I am sad – *head clutched in hands* – bring me joy – *hands extended upwards*; when I am afraid – *hands defend the face* – make me calm – *hands joined in prayer*; when I am grasping – *gripping gesture* – make me generous – *open hands*. And let me offer these hands to you – *offering*.

The new Offertory Prayer speaks of the 'work of our hands'…So the gestures were perfectly appropriate, full of meaning, entirely reverent. And no English inhibitions affected anyone.

As for the dancers, Fr Kevin Donovan explained that

the dance could illustrate a story or express the response of the believer. Just as a church needs a choir to lead but not displace the congregation, so it could have a dance group. The Reigate Liturgical Dance Group illustrated what was in effect the sorrowful mysteries of the rosary. The scourging at the pillar was a frightening imprisonment in grasping hands, conveyed by the simplest of gestures. And it corresponded to what was said in one of the prayers: "Now that the ears of my ears: are awake, and the eyes of my eyes are opened."

There was something suitable about the choice of Notre Dame de France for the dance. First because it is within a stone's throw of Soho, the part of London where the body is abused and sold and exploited. But also because behind the altar stands the tapestry designed by Matisse which shows 'Our Lady of France' surrounded by fabulous beasts, and texts from the Book of Wisdom which tell how Wisdom loved to disport itself. The dance of the children reminded me irresistibly of the patristic idea of Christ as Lord of the Dance, in which Christ leads his people in the Easter dance of salvation. At the wedding feast there will be dancing.

The Month, August 1973

Somebody said that the sisters were going to do a liturgical dance for the golden jubilee of their chapel's dedication. One groaned inwardly at the thought of gimmicky guitars and junior school jingles at Tymawr. Then the afternoon arrived, and the guests and visitors

all met in the chapel in something of the atmosphere of
Parents' Day at school – what with extra chairs and
crowded seating and the girls obviously getting ready to
do something special in bare feet.

Then it started. Within minutes prejudice was calmed
and melted away. It was evident that this liturgical
dance, like much else at Tymawr, was to prove a wonderful experience, telling of truths deeply rooted in our
human condition. Here was the proclamation of the
good news in movement and music. Here was a real live
Paschal dance. As the sisters moved through the various
scenes, so they symbolised situations in life that we
would recognize and know. There was the soul agoniz-
ing in loneliness and despair being soothed and healed
by the wholesomeness of Christ's Spirit. There were
those aching to love and be loved, and finding no one
until they were found by Him to whom they could
respond. Here was the iron-closed group, gripped in the
prison of their own ideals, until the Spirit of Christ
melted them into a loving creative community.

These and other things were there. Loneliness, pain,
despair, hatred, longing, frenzy, all were performed; and
all were transformed when love, joy, trust, peace were
danced. And so life-giving dance moved on, and we
were redeemed, remade and sanctified in Him, the great
Lover.

Bodily movement and music as such may not be
properly contained in words, and so I have not
described the dance, but only what I saw and found
within the dance. However it remains to say that the
sisters did this, as they do so many things, thoroughly
and with a simplicity of spirit that many of us find so

helpful and encouraging. Our thanks are due to them and to their teacher...I am reminded of a very old woman in my parish, who knows nothing of all this but who said to me the other day, "Vicar, I want to dance my way to heaven."

A priest associate of Tymawr Convent

A dancer's body leaps and falls,
and as the move succeeds or fails
   she cannot hide behind her pride
   but openly herself reveals.

No clothes to hide behind upon the cross.
God's nailed and naked dance
   in pain is learning to be still,
   and all its promises fulfil.

No tomb to hide behind but in the dawn,
a body, filled with light,
   will dance among us as we grieve
   and gasp, and believe.

Brian Wren

So many things have happened because other people inspired me. I did a dance recently called *Steal away* and I thought people would come in quietly with gentle circling movements. I simply asked them to come in to the central area and listen to the music. But one small group

came in really burdened and broken. I hadn't suggested
that they do this, but in my own mind were these float-
ing lyrical movements. Yet it was strong and compelling,
and it was their own creation. I learned a lot from that. I
learned to keep quiet. People are amazing.

MARGARET STEVENS

For those who had the power
   of the forest fires that burn
Leaving their source in ashes
   to flush the sky with fire:
Those who a famous urn
   could not contain, whose passion
Brimmed over the deep grave
   and dazzled epitaphs:
For all that have won us wings
   to clear the tops of grief,
My friend who within me laughs
   bids you dance and sing.

Some set out to explore
   earth's limit and little they recked if
Never their feet came near it,
   outgrowing their need for glory:
Some aimed at a small objective
   but the fierce updraught of their spirit
Forced them to the stars.
   Are honoured in public who built
The dam that tamed a river;
   or holding the salient for hours

Against odds, cut off and killed,
   are remembered by one survivor.

All these. But most for those
   whom accident made great.
As a radiant chance encounter
   of cloud and sunlight grows
Immortal on the heart:
   whose gift was the sudden bounty
Of a passing moment, enriches
   the fulfilled eye for ever.
Their spirits float serene
   above time's roughest reaches,
But their seed is in us and over
   our lives they are evergreen.

C. Day Lewis

The
Saint Michael's Dancers

The
Saint Michael's Dancers

On 25th May 1972 a group of dancers first appeared in Coventry Cathedral at a celebration of the Eucharist. The occasion was the tenth anniversary of the consecration of that special place. Uncertain steps were taken that day, but under the direction of Margaret Stevens even the uncertain would be taken up in the vision and purpose she wanted to share – a vision of a community of Christian people coming alive and moving in patterns of prayer and praise, a purpose to release the imagination and to respond from the inner depths to "the great things God has done" (Acts 2.12)…is doing…will do …with us and for us.

The first dance was intended for the ruins of the fourteenth century cathedral, destroyed in the Second World War on the night of 14th November 1940. It was based on an American Indian rain dance, and it proved so effective at rehearsal that falling rain from the canopy of sky above us caused the clergy to move the location just inside the west doors of the new cathedral. The improvised percussion accompaniment to the rhythmic beating of hands on the earth, followed by joyous leaps into the air, must have caused some surprise. Later in the service a contrasting and stately processional to Bach's organ prelude *Wachet auf* surrounded the offerings which were carried up to to a central nave altar by the dancers.

43

Who were these dancers? They were not professionals giving a performance, though some of them had experience of dance. They were members of the cathedral community persuaded by Margaret that it was possible for dance to become worship.

In 1971 Prof. Van C. Kussrow from Indiana had visited Coventry with some of his students to explore ways in which drama and the arts can be part of contemporary worship. He had invited Margaret to lead some sessions on dance, and such was the enthusiasm of the participants that they asked the Canon Pastor of the cathedral for more. It seemed particularly right that a new cathedral should be a place for innovation and experiment – and such dance was certainly new to us.

So it happened that Margaret was asked to tutor us. She began her regular journeys each Monday from Reigate in Surrey to Coventry and back home again on the last train, carrying stereo, cassettes, coloured silks, and whatever else might be needed. There must be something special about the day because the group has continued meeting on Mondays ever since.

Margaret continued with us for more than a year. During that time the group became more stable, with a number of people losing their initial enthusiasm and withdrawing. The serious and disciplined nature of what we were undertaking was established, and the possibilities of future exploration and development were glimpsed.

When Margaret left us to our own devices, she must have known there was a risk of failure. So many groups depend on the dynamism and enthusiasm of their leader to such a degree that when the leader goes the group disintegrates quite quickly. The fact that the Coventry dancers have continued for more than twenty years owes much to the way in which Margaret persuaded and encouraged us and built up our confidence. There was always that innocent and beautiful smile or a warm hug for those who were ready to go with her on the creative journey. She valued us for the particular contributions each of us made, and for the character and quality of our movement, whatever its limitation.

Margaret also used her persuasive powers to get done what had not previously been done – or at least had not been allowed for in the traditions and regulations known to most ecclesiastical authorities. The researches of Prof. John G. Davies, published in 1984 in his book *Liturgical Dance*, have shown that there is more to that tradition than the dualist horror of showing forth the body in such an activity as dance.

The way we move is an expression of what we are and what we might become. So from earliest times movement and dance have formed a vital part of worship. Such movements have been at times wild, ecstatic, charismatic, while at other times they have been carefully shaped and choreographed into dances which explore the deep mysteries of human experience. The tradition of religious dance is both ancient and universal. Surviving records show that Christians danced their worship in the fourth century, though the forms they used are a matter of conjecture. Earlier Jewish traditions also refer to the dance: "Let them praise his name in the dance." (Psalm 149.3)

In our own time this tradition has been revived as the Church seeks to renew its whole life and worship. All kinds of techniques and styles are used: classical, contemporary, folk, jazz, and whatever else may present itself. For the Saint Michael's Dancers choreography is usually evolved through the working sessions of the group, a leader providing initial ideas and directing the process. We do draw upon the tradition, making use of the choral music of English cathedrals, weaving our dances into the liturgical fabric of common prayer, and claiming as our physical space the architectural creation of Sir Basil Spence. We are surrounded by the works of artists who provided the 'jewels in his casket' – Graham Sutherland, John Piper, Elizabeth Frink, Geoffrey Clarke, John Hutton, and others.

Margaret Stevens too is a creative artist who is able to release that creativity in others. She enables us to "enter upon the glorious liberty of the sons and daughters of God" (Romans 8.21). So often in the past the imagination has been stifled by the constraints and fearfulness of those in authority in the Church. Margaret has shown us in her own being and by her skill that dance as much as tapestry or stained glass can give glory to God.

Unfortunately, some of us have become aware in the last few years of the old fearfulness surfacing again. The Christian Dance Fellowship of Britain in its 1990 constitution requires its national committee to make a pledge of support for the doctrine defined in its statement of faith, thus providing support for "the banner we are raising up as evangelicals/charismatics". What could be wrong with that? Surely Christians need to be able to affirm the faith in a clear and uncompromising way. But history shows that whenever doctrines have been defined, usually with the intention of condemning some

heresy, the consequent exclusion of alternative under-
standings and expressions of truth narrowed both the
faith and spirit of orthodox believers.

Did Jesus require his disciples to sign a doctrinal statement before they could follow him? No. They came as
they were with a baggage of religious convictions and
prejudices which were transformed by experience on the
journey of faith, and they came with flawed human
natures as real as their potential to be witnesses to the
truth.

When we are confronted with demands for a declara-
tion of faith, we should not be afraid to "give an account
of the hope that is in us" (1 Peter 3.15), but we should
recognize that truth is always greater than the words
which try to express it. Dancers should particularly be
able to go beyond the limits of language as they seek to
communicate something of the divine mystery and face
the challenge of paradox. As Prof. James Dunn says in
The Evidence for Jesus, "My truth and my confession and
my liturgy can never be the truth, the confession, the
liturgy. It is always provisional and approximate and
inadequate in relation to the greater reality which
human words and actions can never encapsulate or fully
express."

This may seem something of a digression from the
subject of the imaginative freedom of the choreographer
and dancer, but questions have been asked about
whether someone who is not a convinced Christian can
be part of our dance worship group, about whether
music which is secular in intention and theme may be
used for such dance, and whether certain techniques
and styles derived from non-Christian sources (such as

yoga breathing exercises and Sufi or Israeli circle dances) ought to be permitted in a Christian context. Of course there can be discussion of these questions and different points of view, but we would not want to impose answers by an appeal solely to personal revelation or received dogma.

The Saint Michael's Dancers have been involved with three Mind-Body-Spirit Festivals at Olympia in London, rather in the tradition of the apostle Paul preaching in Athens. We were also asked to contribute an Egyptian sacred dance as part of a performance of Verdi's *Aida* by the Leamington Spa Opera Group. Of course these occasions were not specifically Christian in form or content, but it did not seem to us that they were anti-Christian, nor that God is absent from what may seem to be 'merely' secular.

We would not wish to make a rigid separation of sacred from secular. The physical universe of which we are a part is not in itself evil, though of course any skill can be used to evil ends. So dance for liturgy needs to be dance of the whole person, without censorship of certain parts of the body or particular styles of movement of which we are afraid. Our experiences of life are reflected in our bodies. We are called to offer the whole of ourselves to God, not selected fragments.

We would need to distinguish between a lazy acceptance of the second-rate (often excused by indulgent church groups who will not criticise what is bad because the people responsible are claiming that they are saying or doing what God has directly told them to do) and a disciplined effort to provide as much of the first-rate as one can. The second-rate must not be allowed to slip by as 'the inspiration of the Spirit'. Even if the Spirit is a gift, and the moment of real communication cannot be guaranteed or predicted, the possibility of such marvellous moments occurring is enhanced by our disciplined understanding and skills. Margaret approaches the work with such practical good sense that there is no fear of the dance leading into realms of unreality and aimless fantasy.

Some dancers seem unable to face the rigours of criticism. They do not wish to interfere with what they believe to be the free and individual impulses of the Spirit or to exert any rational control. Surely the Spirit leads us to "a right judgment in all things" (Collect for Whit Sunday in the *Book of Common Prayer*) so that we may distinguish what has artistic integrity from what is cheap, easy, and banal.

Margaret helps us to reach that 'right judgment'. She does not confuse what feels good with what really is good dance. She has a dread of those who waft about with eyes half closed, swathed in emotional warmth. She would often say, "That was dreadful, dears," and we knew she was right. But her criticisms were not marks of failure. Far from finishing us off, they renewed our determination to get it right. Such boundless energy would flow from her that a matching response was evoked from the tiring troops.

In February 1991 it was inspiring to find Margaret with undiminished vigour leading an afternoon of dance on the theme of the Tree of Life at St James's Church, Piccadilly, in London, where Donald Reeves, her old friend and supporter, is now the Rector. Many of the present generation of dance leaders there had learned their first and most important lessons from her. Yet they were left gasping whilst she was ready for more. "We've only just started!" she cried. The energies drawn upon in her dances are as much emotional as physical – a whole range of emotions that we had forgotten, or had preferred to hide away.

Yet always the practical good sense was there. I remember her instruction to those about to create a new dance: "Don't keep talking about it – do it!" It is worth exploring this, for dance in worship is not meant to 'illustrate' a sermon or a Bible text in a literal way. It may of course be a response to such words, but there is something which communicates through the patterns, movements and shapes of human bodies which cannot translate into or be directly derived from other words, any more than an organ prelude can be communicated by the organist writing an explanatory paragraph. Our failure to grasp this perhaps owes something to the way in which our worship is so saturated with words. Where can we find a silence strong enough to stem the flow of words? Where but in Taizé is there an instinct to suppress every useless word? When we dance, it is the *dance* that is primary: it is not an optional extra, as though it were really the words which were conveying the message. When this is not understood, the dance becomes an extra ingredient in the service, needing special permission or explanation or careful restriction, because it might otherwise distract from the real business of 'saying Mass' or 'preaching the Word'.

The Saint Michael's Dancers have tried to promote the dance as a valid act of worship in itself, as something which will release the creative imagination and embody

the ultimate realities in ways which bring about corres-
ponding physical and emotional responses in the bodies
of those who are watching. You cannot *explain* all this:
you can only lure people into the *experience*. Sadly there
is still resistance to putting your body where your words
are – or where your faith is. So we need to find new
ways of engaging the physical potential of those who are
'the body of Christ', new ways to embody the faith we
experience as our own and would share with others.
"… the Gospel is not fundamentally an idea but an
action, a deliverance, and no action can be bodiless in
human experience: the Gospel must bring good news
and liberation to our bodies or it will not liberate anything." (Prof. James B. Nelson, *Embodiment*)

Our second leader, Wendy Bunn, came to us in 1973,
when our technique was proving inadequate for the
dances we wanted to create. She encouraged us to
attempt more difficult movements and more complex
choreography, which it would have been easier and less
challenging to avoid. She restored some of the discipline
of Margaret's era, which we had allowed to slide some-
what.

It was during this period that the group became ecumenical and international. Stillness and silence is char-
acteristic of Quaker worship, yet a Quaker who joined
us was fully committed to the dance. International visitors to the cathedral were able to join us for a year or
more. We had dancers from the United States,
Switzerland, Sweden, and elsewhere. A number of men
also participated. All these dimensions made for an
offering that was more complete.

On occasion we have been able to create liturgies

which specifically focused on the dance. There was the *Party at Bethlehem* in 1975, an Epiphany theme in which the three gifts of the wise men became three dances; *The Way of Reconciliation* for the fortieth anniversary of the bombing of the old cathedral, which reflected on destruction, crucifixion, and new life arising; a *Dance Celebration* in 1987 exploring themes of inner struggle, the cry out of the depths, and consolation, as well as a healing dance which led to an act of prayer with anointing.

Another *Dance Celebration* in 1993 marked with thanksgiving the twenty-one years' life and work of The St Michael's Dancers. It featured dances choreographed by the three leaders of the group over this period.

Ample space for these dances was provided by moving hundreds of chairs so that a central nave arena was surrounded on three sides by chairs for the congregation (the dancers occupying the back rows) and the other side open to the chancel where the ministers and choir remained in their usual places. Four candles marked off the special place in which the dancers would move.

I myself became the third leader of the Dancers in 1983, and although we have faced fluctuations of numbers owing to pregnancy, illness, and domestic crises, the group has continued to thrive and meet new challenges. I recall Jeanne Fuller, a dance leader and friend from Darien, Connecticut, when we were hesitant about an Easter tour to the States, writing to us: "Make practical plans to come. Between now and then, and with the Lord, we will help work for that reality. Don't worry about the money. As long as it is in all our hearts it will work out." And so, incredibly, it did, and we were able to share our experience of dance worship with many enthusiastic Americans.

Another triumph of hope and will over practical problems was our dance for the *Service of Remembrance and Reconciliation* on 14th November 1990, in the presence of the Queen Mother. The dance, called *Ruined and Rebuilt*, was done to Aaron Copland's music, *Fanfare for the Common Man*, played by the Fine Arts Brass Ensemble. Dramatic architectural shapes were formed from the bodies of four dancers in purple. Four others in red advanced upon them, twisting and moving flame-like between and around them, pushing them into semi-collapsed or melted forms. The red group sank down, only to rise again, the holy and life-giving spirit at the heart of their circular shape. The group reached out to invite the purple dancers to enter their shape. There was a momentary glimpse of Coventry's three spires formed by arms reaching high, and then the whole shape began to revolve. The dancers took up red and purple ribbons. (The purple ones had been flown in from Ireland the day before and stitched together overnight.) The ribbons fanned out and then rippled behind the alternating colours of dancers running down the central aisle of the cathedral to the great west screen.

Many people who do not always understand or respond to dance worship said how much it added to the dramatic shape of the liturgy and what a spectacular climax it provided, with its combination of movement, music, colour and pattern.

We had learned a few days previously that Aaron Copland's ninetieth birthday was also on 14th

November 1990. It was to be his last. We also discovered that the music had been written as a tribute to all involved in the action of the Second World War, particularly those who "perform no deeds of heroism on the battlefield but who share the labours, sorrows and hopes of those who strive for victory."

The recently acclaimed dancer and choreographer, Stephen Petronio, presents us with a radical challenge: "I don't even like dance because usually it is meant to show the pretty side of things, and if it doesn't, well then you're fighting an uphill battle." The Saint Michael's Dancers have attempted to reflect more than just 'the pretty side of things', not by abandoning the light and hope of the Gospel, but by a serious grappling with the darker realities of human experience. Only so can we come to a deeper encounter with God than can be known by the exuberance of the enthusiast or by the desire for feelings of reassurance.

We have created a number of 'darker' dances. In December 1981 we presented a picture of exclusion and loneliness with a solo male dancer set against the closed forms of the group. The music for this was *Man on the Corner* by the rock group *Genesis*. Then we responded to the troubles in Ireland with a Lament for a mother whose children had been taken from her. The music for this was the *Theme from Harry's Game* by Paul Brennan, sung in Gaelic by a young student. In 1987 we made a more violent *Dance of Inner Struggle* using a dramatic anthem for choir and organ by Neil Cox called *War in Heaven*. We used a length of black chain which at times bound the dancers, from which they escaped and with which they made strange triangular patterns. In

October 1989 we did a *Fragile Dance* to the recorded music of Sting singing *Fragile*. It was our contribution to a special service for a group at the cathedral studying sexuality. It showed how, when my own pain causes me to reach out and touch others, I cannot know if they will bear the burden of knowing me, of holding me. How fragile we are.

We continue to provide workshops and to respond to requests for contributions to worship whenever we are asked. We still want to find new ways for congregations to move and in simple ways to echo the dancers' praise, the praise of God which is the focus of all our creative work.

We trust that we will *persuade* those who are hesitant about taking their first steps in a dance which is worship. We want to be *liberators* and bring a release of imaginative gifts that are so often locked inside people. We expect to continue a *disciplined* approach to the work, without which we cannot hope to make progress. And we want *practical good sense* rather than pious platitudes to inform those who are struggling.

Those four sentences come to mind spontaneously as I think again of Margaret Stevens and her contribution to the beginnings of the revival of movement and dance as worship in this country, and in particular her contribution as the founder of The Saint Michael's Dancers at Coventry. What better tribute could there be than a movement that continues and grows in the same spirit which she embodies so wonderfully.

JOHN BRASSINGTON

Acknowledgments

Thanks are due to those who have given permission for copyright material to be reproduced in this book. If anyone's rights have been infringed – we have done our best to trace every source – we can but apologize and promise to put matters right in any future edition. The references which follow are in the order in which the material appears in the book.

The quotation by Anna Primavesi comes from her article 'Song of Gaia' in the magazine *Resurgence* no. 146, 1991.

The poem by Harold Morland is entitled Song Thrush. It was a gift to the publisher of this book and is acknowledged with gratitude.

The quotation by Tim Gorringe comes from his article 'Sacred Space: Traditions in Conflict' in the magazine *Church Building*, Autumn 1992.

Isodora Duncan is quoted in Margot Fonteyn's book, *The Magic of Dance*, BBC Publications, 1979.

The quotation by the Librarian of Westminster Abbey is from a guide book to the building.

The poem by Sr Benedicta, of the Society of the Sacred Cross at Tymawr, Monmouth, was a personal gift to Margaret Stevens, and is quoted with gratitude.

I have not been able to trace the source of the quotation by Ernest Hemingway.

The quotation by Thomas Traherne comes from his *Meditations*.

Cheryl Cooke's contribution comes from a personal letter and is used with thanks.

Similarly with gratitude – the quotation from a personal letter from Graham Suter.

The passage by Havelock Ellis is from his *Affirmations* on Nietzsche, published by Constable, 1926.

The contributions of Wendy Bunn and Graham Hill are from personal letters and used with thanks.

The summary of Rodin's philosophy is from Camille Monclair's *Rodin, the man and his ideas*.

The quotations by Aidan Kavanagh are from his book, *The Elements of Rite*, Pueblo Publishing Company, New York, 1982.

The quotations by Donald Reeves are from his book, *For God's Sake*, Fount, 1988.

I am afraid I have been unable to trace the quotation from Patrick White.

The poem by Thomas Blackburn is entitled 'The Spirit Dances', originally published by Peter Owen and incorporated into his *Selected Poems*, Hutchinson of London, 1975.

The poem by Elizabeth Jennings, 'The Dancers', can be

found in her *Collected Poems*, published by Carcanet in 1967.

The paragraph by Sam Keen is from his book, *To a Dancing God*, Fontana, 1971.

Laudato Si, O mi Signore is a song based on the famous prayer attributed to St Francis of Assisi.

Janet Morley's prayer was originally written for Margaret Stevens and is to be found in her book, *All Desires Known*, SPCK, 1992.

The paragraph by Keith Plaister is from a personal letter, and is acknowledged with thanks.

The extract by Vaslav Nijinsky is from his Diary, published by Gollancz, 1937.

The anonymous poem, entitled *You Dance*, was sent to Margaret Stevens by a theological student at Westcott House, Cambridge, after she had spent Holy Week with the college one year.

The poem by James Elroy Flecker comes from his *Collected Poems*, published by Martin Secker.

I have been unable to trace the source of the quotation by Jiddu Krishnamurti.

I have lost my copy of *The Month* for August 1973 and apologize to the writer of the article for not mentioning him or her by name.

The account of the dance at the golden jubilee of the dedication of the chapel at Tymawr was published in the magazine of the Community.

'A Time to Dance' by C. Day Lewis can be found in his *Complete Poems*, published by Sinclair-Stevenson in 1992.

'A Dancer's Body Leaps and Falls' is part of a hymn of that name by Brian Wren in his collection *Bring Many Names*, Hope Publishing Company, Carol Stream, Illinois, 1989, distributed by the Oxford University Press and used with their permission.